STONY POINT

Introduction to Salesforce Analytics
Building Reports and Dashboards

(SPRD-101)

Author: Steve Wasula

1

Agenda

- Agenda & Course Overview
- Introduction to GenWatt
- Setting up a Practice Site
- Salesforce.com Object Model
- Schema Builder
- List Views
- Reports
  - Report Folders
  - Tabular Reports
  - Summary Reports
  - Matrix Reports
  - Date Filters
  - Join Reports
  - Report Charts
  - Bucket Fields
  - Report Summary Fields
  - Conditional Highlighting
  - Custom Report Types
  - Report Scheduling
- Dashboards
  - Folders
  - Components
  - Running User
  - Dashboard Scheduling

2

Course Overview

- About this Course
- About the Instructor
- Introductions
- Course Structure
  - Introduce concept & technology
  - Exercise to use concept in system
- Housekeeping

3

Business Scenario: GenWatt

GenWatt currently sells generators to large companies and has been using Salesforce for six months. Generally, they are happy with Salesforce and think that they are getting value from it.

They feel that their sales processes have improved and the pipeline is growing, but upper management isn't sure . In addition, some members of management fear that not all users are adopting the system.

You have been asked to build reports and dashboards to measure user adoption, sales performance and help segment customers and prospects.

4

4

Your Practice Site

For this hands-on training class, you will need to set up a **Salesforce Developer Edition** to perform the class exercises.

The **Salesforce Developer Edition** is a completely free testing environment that contains a minimal amount of test data and will be available to you forever.

Perform the following steps to set up a Developer Edition for hands-on exercises in this class.

5

5

Practice Site Action Steps

1. Go to http://developer.force.com
2. Click on the link "Get a Free Developer Edition"

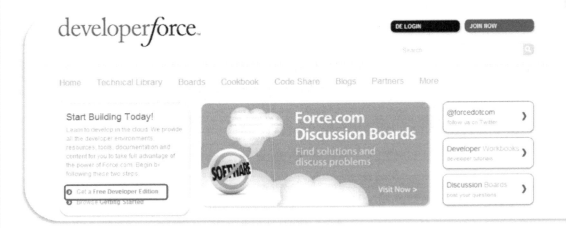

6

Practice Site Action Steps

3. Fill out the form provided to set up your developer's edition and click **Submit**

*Username Format: **firstname.lastname@sprd101.dev**

7

Practice Site Action Steps

4. Check your email inbox associated with your developer edition

5. Click on the link within the email from Salesforce to login to your developer edition

```
Welcome to Force.com Developer Edition.
Dear Dana Cowden,

Your user name is below. Note that it is in the form of an email address:

User name: dana@training.com.dev

You'll be asked to set a password and password question and answer when you first log in.
Passwords are case sensitive.
Your password question and answer will be used if you forget your password. Make sure to choose a password question and
answer that you will easily remember.

Click https://login.salesforce.com?c=114m45n2Bp8yq4eYXCM2L7Ej5R3swJzRTga3IfMZadIgiptjd6.j5Ljh1GnOugvI4I5JRbmKRImg%3D%3D to
log in now.
```

8

Practice Site Action Steps

6. Create your new password and security question
7. Click **Save** to log in to your new developer edition

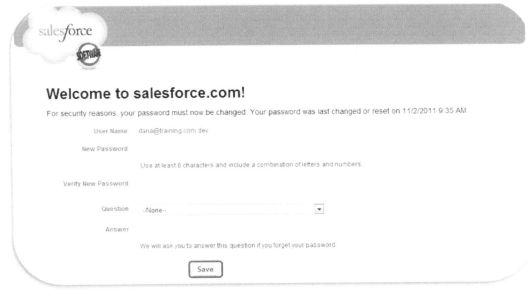

Salesforce Object Model

- **Universal Objects**
  - Accounts, Contacts, Tasks, Events
- **Sales Objects**
  - Opportunities, Products, Price Books, Quotes
- **Customer Service Objects**
  - Cases, Solutions
- **Marketing Objects**
  - Leads, Campaigns
- **Custom Objects**
- **Entity Relationship Diagram**
  - http://www.salesforce.com/us/developer/docs/api/Content/ sforce_api_erd_majors.htm

_____

_____

_____

_____

_____

_____

_____

Universal Objects

- Account
  - An organization
- Contact
  - A person, usually associated with an Account
- Task
  - A "to do" list item
- Event
  - A scheduled activity
  - Normally has activities and specific attendees

11

_____

_____

_____

_____

_____

_____

_____

Sales Objects

- # Opportunity
  - A chance to generate revenue

- # Product
  - A good or service sold

- # Price Book
  - A catalog of products

- # Quote
  - A price given to a customer or prospect

Customer Service Objects

- Case
  - Something that needs to get resolved

- Solution
  - A knowledge base article that can be used to resolve a Case

13

Marketing Objects

- **Lead**
  - Unqualified

- **Campaign**
  - A list of Leads and Contacts

Custom Objects

- Any object not included with Salesforce
- Facilitate the capture of unique, business specific data
- Best Practices
  - Always use Account for any organization
  - Always use Contact for any person
  - Always use Case for issue tracking

Object Relationships

- Object can be related to one another
- Relationships are created when a relationship field is added to an object
- Two types of relationship fields:
  - Lookup
  - Master Detail
- The object with the lookup field on it is referred to as the child in the relationship
- The object being related is referred to as the parent in the relationship
- Lookup and Master Detail fields have similar but different characteristics

_____

_____

_____

_____

_____

_____

_____

Determining Object Relationships

- Fields
    - You can determine the relationships between objects by navigating the object customization screen and looking at all the field definitions
    - Master Detail relationships will be shown in the main list of Objects

Action		Label	Installed Package	Master Object	Deployed	Description
Edit		Activity	LMS ILT	Development Plan	✓	
Edit		Assignment	LMS Learning	Transcript, Training User License	✓	LMS Consumer Application
Edit		Cancellation Policy	LMS ILT		✓	
Edit		Cart	LMS Learning		✓	LMS Consumer Application
Edit		Catalog	LMS Learning		✓	
Edit		Catalog Account	LMS Learning	Account, Catalog	✓	

- ## You can also utilize the Schema Builder
    - Allows you to create a visual diagram of object relationships
    - Allows you to edit objects

_____

_____

_____

_____

_____

_____

_____

Exercise: Schema Builder

Action Steps:

1. Navigate to the Schema Builder. Path: Setup -> App Setup -> Schema Builder
2. From the menu on the left, make sure the Objects tab is selected
3. From the drop down list named Select from, make sure All Objects is selected
4. Check the Clear All link to deselect all objects and clear the screen
5. Add the following Objects to the Schema Builder diagram by checking the box next to the Object:
   a. Account
   b. Case
   c. Contact
   d. Opportunity
   e. Opportunity Product
6. When you feel like you understand the relationships between these Objects, click the Close button to close the Schema Builder
   a. You cannot save diagrams

_____

_____

_____

_____

_____

_____

_____

_____

List Views

- Available on most tabs
- Show only records of one type of object
- Are customizable
  - Filters
  - Columns
- Provide nice navigation features
  - Edit returns to list
  - View provides a breadcrumb back to list
- Can be built by end users
- Can be secured individually

19

19

Exercise: List Views

Action Steps:

1. Create a new List View for Accounts
2. Navigate to the Sales application and then to the Accounts tab
3. Create a new view by clicking on the Create New View link

4. Choose the following options
   a. View Name: All Accounts
   b. View Unique Name: All_Accounts
   c. Filter By Owner: All Accounts
   d. Select whatever you would like to display in the Select Fields to Display area
5. Make the View visible to all users in the Restrict Visibility area
6. Save the View

Reports Overview

 ## What is a Report?

- A Report shows a set of data with something in common
- A List Report displays a simple list of records
- A Summary Report displays records with up to three levels of grouping
- A Matrix Report displays records in a 2 x 2 grid format, similar to an Excel pivot table
- A Join Report allows you to run multiple reports at the same time as long as they have a common key
- A Report always shows real time data

21

21

Reports Security

The information displayed in reports is data to which the running user has access. This may include:

- Records owned by the User
- Records shared with the User
- Records owned by or shared with people below the running User in the Role Hierarchy
- Fields that are visible or editable to you

In general, if a User can search for and access the records in Salesforce, they will be able to report on them.

Report Folders

- In order to run a Report, the User must have access to the Report Folder in which the Report is stored
- Report Folders Settings:
  - Public Folder Access:
    - Read Only
      - Users with access to the folder can run Reports in the folder but cannot modify the Reports
    - Read / Write
      - Users with access to the folder can run Reports in the folder and can also modify the Reports and save them back into the folder
      - Users with access to the folder can create new Reports and save them to the folder
  - Accessibility
    - This folder is accessible by all Users
      - Every User in Salesforce can see the report folder
      - When running reports in the folder, standard record security rules still apply
    - This folder is hidden from all Users
      - Only System Administrator profile can see the folder
    - This folder is accessible from only the following Users
      - Only named Groups, Roles & Roles & Subordinates can see the report folder
      - When running reports in the folder, standard record security rules still apply

Exercise: Create a Report Folder

Action Steps:

1. Create a new Report Folder to hold all the GenWatt reports
2. Navigate to the Reports tab
3. Click on the New Reports Folder link

4. Choose the following options
   a. Report Folder Label: GenWatt Reports
   b. Folder Unique Name: GenWatt_Reports
   c. Public Folder Access: Read Only
   d. This folder is accessible by all users
5. Don't add any Reports to the folder at this time
6. Save the folder

Standard Reports

- Salesforce comes with a large number of Standard Reports
- Designed to be templates for the System Administrator to use
- Stored in Standard Report Folders
- Cannot be modified
  - Can be customized and saved as new custom reports
- Are not searchable
- **Best Practice**: Hide all Standard Report Folders from all Users
  - System Administrator will still be able to see all folders and reports within them

25

Exercise: Hide Standard Reports

Action Steps:

1. Hide all Standard Reports from all Users by hiding the standard report folders

2. Navigate to the Reports tab

Reports Terminology

- Report Type
  - The data that will be available to the report
- Report Format
  - The way the data will display on the report
- Scope
  - Always configurable filters at the top of the report
- Custom Filters
  - Criteria that is used to filter the records in a report

27

_____

_____

_____

_____

_____

_____

_____

Tabular Report

- Tabular reports are the simplest reports
- Consist simply of an ordered set of fields in columns, with each matching record listed in a row.
- Tabular reports are best for creating lists of records or a list with a single grand total.
- Can't be used to:
  - Create groups of data or charts
  - Can't be used in dashboards unless rows are limited.

28

_____

_____

_____

_____

_____

_____

_____

Exercise: Create a Tabular Report

Action Steps:

1. Create a new Tabular Report listing all the Account records
2. Navigate to the Reports tab and click on New Report button

   Reports & Dashboards   [New Report...] [New Dashboard...]

   Folders   All Folders   [New Report...]

3. Search for Accounts, select the Accounts type and create the report by clicking the Create button

   ### Create New Report

   Select Report Type

   Q Quick Find

   ⊟ 🗀 Accounts & Contacts
      Accounts
      Contacts & Accounts
      Accounts with Partners
      Account with Account Teams
      Accounts with Contact Roles

   Preview

   Account Report

   Account Owner

   Joe Johnson
   Shelly Smith
   Tom Thompson

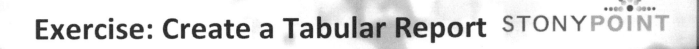
Action Steps:

4. Add the following columns to the report:
   a. Account Owner, Account Name, Type, Rating, Last Activity, Last Modified Date, Billing State/Province, Website

5. Change the Scope to:
   a. Show: All Accounts
   b. Range: All Time

6. Run the report by clicking the Run Report button

7. Save the report by clicking the Save As button

8. Make sure to save the report in the GenWatt Reports folder

9. Click the Save and Return to Report button

Summary Report

- Allow groupings
- Allow subtotals
- Allow charts
- Can be used to populate a dashboard component

Exercise: Create a Summary Report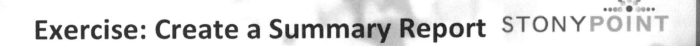

Action Steps:

1. Create a new Summary Report listing all the Account records with open or closed Opportunities
2. Navigate to the Reports tab and click on New Report button
3. Search for Opportunities, select the Opportunities report type and create the report by clicking the Create button
4. Add the following columns to the report:
   a. Opportunity Name, Opportunity Owner, Close Date, Stage, Amount
5. Change the Scope to:
   a. Show: All Opportunities
   b. Range: All Time
6. Change the Report Format to Summary
7. Group the Report by Account Name
8. Group the Report by Won
9. Summarize the Sum of the Amount Field
10. Run the report by clicking the Run Report button
11. Save the report by clicking the Save As button
12. Name the report All Opportunities by Account
13. Make sure to save the report in the GenWatt reports folder
14. Click the Save and Return to Report button

Matrix Report

- Matrix reports are similar to summary reports
- Allow you to group and summarize data by both rows and columns.
- Similar to an Excel pivot table
  - Don't allow pivoting
- Allow charts
- Can be used as the source report for dashboard components.

_____

_____

_____

_____

_____

_____

_____

Exercise: Create a Matrix Report

Action Steps:

1. Create a new Matrix Report listing all the open Opportunity records grouped by Owner, Quarter and Month

2. Navigate to the Reports tab and click on New Report button

3. Search for Opportunities, select the Opportunities type and create the report by clicking the Create button

4. Change the Scope to:

    a. Show: All Opportunities

    b. Opportunity Status: Open

    c. Range: All Time

5. Change the Report Format to Matrix

6. In the left grouping area, group the Report by Opportunity Owner

7. In the top grouping area, group Close Date

    a. Change the date grouping to Calendar Month

8. Using the Show menu, remove the Details from the report

34

Exercise: Create a Matrix Report

Action Steps:

9. Drag the Amount field into the Matrix and choose Sum as the summary type
10. Using the Show menu, remove the Details from the report
11. Run the report by clicking the Run Report button
12. Save the report by clicking the Save As button
13. Name the report Open Opportunities by Month
14. Make sure to save the report in the GenWatt Reports folder
15. Click the Save and Return to Report button

Business Scenario: Matrix Report

Your sales department is very excited about the Matrix report you just created for them. They have asked for what seems like a simple enhancement: Since a Matrix report supports 2 x 2 grouping, can you group Close Date by Calendar Quarter then by Calendar month and also include it in the report details?

Simple answer: No.

Happy Customer Answer: Yes, this can be accomplished because Salesforce provides the Close Date as multiple fields in reports.

Dates

- ## Date Grouping
  - Salesforce supports automatic grouping of dates into days, weeks, months, quarters, years.
    - Automatically supports Fiscal Year and Calendar Year
- ## Special Date Filters
  - Yesterday, Today, Tomorrow,
  - Last Week, Last Month, Last Quarter, Last Year
  - Next Week, Next Month, Last Quarter, Next Year
  - This Week, This Month, This Quarter, This Year
  - Last *n* Days, Last *n* Months, Last *n* Years
  - Next *n* Days, Next *n* Months, Next *n* Years

Exercise: Modify a Matrix Report

Action Steps:

1. Navigate to the Reports tab and find the Open Opportunities by Month report
2. Edit the Report
3. In the top grouping area, drag one of the Close Month field below the existing Close Date grouping
    a. Change the Close Date date grouping to Calendar Quarter
    b. Change the Close Month grouping to Calendar Month
4. Using the Show menu, add the Details from the report
5. Drag the Close Date (2) field into the details section of the report
6. Run the report by clicking the Run Report button
7. Save the report by clicking the Save button
8. Change the name of the report to Open Opportunities by Quarter & Month
9. Click the Save and Return to Report button

Join Report

- Let you create multiple report blocks from multiple report types
- Overcome a long standing reporting limitation in Salesforce
  - Tabular, Summary and Matrix can only report down one branch of the tree
- Creates up to 3 related blocks of data
  - Each block acts like a "sub-report,"
  - Has it own fields, columns, sorting, and filtering.
  - All blocks must have at least one common field to group them together

_____

_____

_____

_____

_____

_____

_____

GenWatt wants to better understand all their customers. They would like a report showing all Accounts, all Contacts associated with those Accounts, all Opportunities and all Cases across all customers and prospects.

Solution: Join Report

40

Exercise: Create a Join Report

Action Steps:

1. Create a new Join Report listing all the Accounts & Contacts, Opportunities and Cases

2. Navigate to the Reports tab and click on New Report button

3. Search for Account, select the Contacts & Accounts type and create the report by clicking the Create button

4. Change the Scope to:

    a. Show: All Accounts

    b. Range: All Time

5. Remove all but the following columns from the report: First Name, Last Name

6. Change the Report Format to Joined

7. Add another report by clicking the Add Report Type button

41

41

Exercise: Create a Join Report

Action Steps:

8. Select the Opportunities type
9. Remove all but the following columns from the Opportunities section: Opportunity Name, Opportunity Owner, Stage, Close Date, Amount
10. Change the Scope to:
    a. Show: All opportunities
    b. Range: All Time
11. Summarize the Sum of the Amount field
12. Add another report by clicking the Add Report Type button
13. Search for Case, select the Cases type and click the OK button
14. Change the Scope to:
    a. Show: All Cases
    b. Units: Days
    c. Range: All Time
15. The Cases section should contain the following columns: Subject, Case Owner, Status, Date/Time Opened

_____

_____

_____

_____

_____

_____

_____

Exercise: Create a Join Report

Action Steps:

16. Choose to group by report by dragging the Account Name field from the Common Fields area in the fields pane on the left to the grouping area on the report

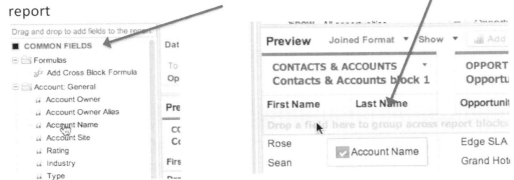

17. Run the report by clicking the Run Report button

18. Save the report by clicking the Save button

19. Name the report All Accounts, Contacts, Opps & Cases

20. Make sure to save the report in the GenWatt Reports folder

21. Click the Save and Close button

43

Report Filters

- Used in addition to Report Scope
- Used to restrict the data that is shown on a report
- Each report can have up to 10 custom filters
- Support the special date filters
- Can use complex filter logic such as AND, OR, NOT
- A User must have the Customize Reports Profile permission enabled to create or edit report filters

_____

_____

_____

_____

_____

_____

_____

Exercise: Create a Report with Filters

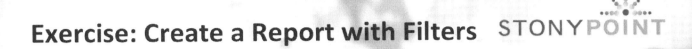

Action Steps:

1. Create a new Summary Report listing all the Over
2. Navigate to the Reports tab and click on New Report button
3. Search for Opportunities, select the Opportunities type and create the report by clicking the Create button
4. Leave all the default columns on the report
5. Change the Scope to:
   a. Show: All Opportunities
   b. Opportunity Status: Open
   c. Range: All Time
6. Change the Report Format to Summary
7. Group the Report by Opportunity Owner
8. Add a Report Filter by clicking the Add button at the top and adding a Field Filter
   a. Close Date less than today
   b. Click the OK button
9. Run the report by clicking the Run Report button
10. Save the report by clicking the Save As button
11. Name the report Overdue Opportunities
12. Make sure to save the report in the GenWatt Reports folder
13. Click the Save and Return to Report button

Report Charts

- Summary and Matrix reports allow the creation of a chart
- The chart can be placed at the top or bottom of the report
- The chart can be sized by the report developer
  - Use big charts when reports have a good amount of data
  - Use smaller charts when the report doesn't have much data
- **Best Practice**: Use as small a chart as possible

46

Exercise: Create a Report Chart

Action Steps:

1. Create a new Summary Report listing all the open Opportunity records
2. Navigate to the Reports tab and click on New Report button
3. Search for Opportunities, select the Opportunities type and create the report by clicking the Create button
4. Leave all the selected columns
5. Change the Scope to:
   a. Show: All Opportunities
   b. Opportunity Status: Open
   c. Range: All Time
6. Change the Report Format to Summary
7. Group the Report by Stage
8. Click the Add Chart button

_____

_____

_____

_____

_____

_____

_____

Exercise: Create a Report Chart

Action Steps:

9. Select a Pie Chart

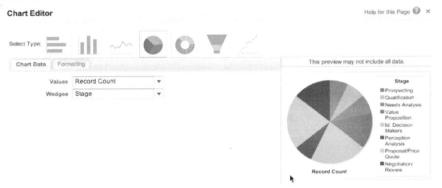

10. Run the report by clicking the Run Report button

11. Save the report by clicking the Save As button

12. Name the report One Opportunities by Stage

13. Make sure to save the report in the GenWatt Reports folder

14. Click the Save and Return to Report button

Bucket Fields

- Allow dynamic grouping of fields at a report level
- Eliminates the need to create formula fields on objects
- Example:
  - Annual Revenue > 50M = "Big"
  - Annual Revenue > 10M < 50M = "Medium"
  - Annual Revenue < 10M = "Small"

_____

_____

_____

_____

_____

_____

_____

Business Scenario: Bucket Fields

STONYPOINT

GenWatt just signed a promotional deal with a movie studio to sponsor the soon to be released remake of Goldilocks and the Three Bears. As part of the promotion, the GenWatt marketing department wants to segment the existing customer base and send them promotional material such as shirts and passes to attend movie premieres. The quality of the material depends on the size of the customer. Marketing wants to you segment the customer base as follows:

- < $5,000,000 in revenue : Baby Bear
- > $5,000,000 < $10,000,000 in revenue: Mama Bear
- > $10,000,000 in revenue: Papa Bear

50

Exercise: Create Bucket Fields

STONYPOINT

Action Steps:

1. Create a new Summary Report listing all the Account records so we can bucket Accounts by revenue

2. Navigate to the Reports tab and click on New Report button

3. Search for Accounts, select the Contacts & Accounts type and create the report by clicking the Create button

4. Ensure the report has the following columns:
   a. Account Name, Annual Revenue, First Name, Last Name, Email

5. Change the Scope to:
   a. Show: All accounts
   b. Range: All Time

6. Click on the Annual Revenue field drop down menu and click on Bucket this Field

_____

_____

_____

_____

_____

_____

_____

Exercise: Create Bucket Fields

Action Steps:

Edit Bucket Field   Help for this

ⓘ Use bucket fields to group, filter, or arrange report data. Create multiple buckets in this bucket field to group your report records.

Source Column: Annual Revenue ▼

Bucket Field Name: | Goldilocks   ⓘ

Define Ranges ⓘ

	Range		Name
	<=	5,000,000	Baby Bear
Add ▶			
	> 5,000,000 to	10,000,000	Mama Bear
Add ▶			Delete
	>	10,000,000	Papa Bear

☑ Treat empty **Annual Revenue** values in the report as zeros.

OK   Cancel

Exercise: Create Bucket Fields

Action Steps:

7. Change the Report Format to Summary
8. Group the Report by the Goldilocks Field
9. Run the report by clicking the Run Report button
10. Save the report by clicking the Save As button
11. Name the report Goldilocks Promotion
12. Make sure to save the report in the GenWatt Reports folder
13. Click the Save and Return to Report button

53

Custom Summary Fields

- Allow complex calculations across multiple records in a report
- Available on Summary, Matrix and Join Reports
  - On Join Reports, can only calculate in a single block
- Support Sum, Largest Value, Smallest Value and Average calculations
- Can reference number, currency, percent, and checkbox fields
  - Can reference rollup summary and formula fields on the object
- Cannot reference another summary formula
  - Must do entire calculation in one formula
  - No intermediate steps
- There is a maximum of 5 custom summary formulas per report

54

Business Scenario: Custom Summary Fields

GenWatt would like to know what percentage of their Opportunities are being closed and lost versus being closed and won. This cannot be accomplished with a simple formula because the calculation needs to be performed across multiple records at once.

_____

_____

_____

_____

_____

_____

_____

Exercise: Custom Summary Fields

Action Steps:

1. Create a new Summary Report listing all Closed Opportunity records
2. Navigate to the Reports tab and click on New Report button
3. Search for Opportunity, select the Opportunities type and create the report by clicking the Create button
4. Change the Scope to:
   a. Show: All Opportunities
   b. Opportunity Status: Closed
   c. Range: All Time
5. Ensure the report has the following columns in order:
   a. Opportunity Owner, Opportunity Name, Close Date, Stage, Amount
6. Change the Report Format to Summary
7. Group the Report by Opportunity Owner
8. Choose to Summarize the Sum of the Amount field

_____

_____

_____

_____

_____

_____

_____

Exercise: Custom Summary Fields STONYPOINT

Action Steps:

9. From the fields pane on the left, double click on the Add Formula menu item

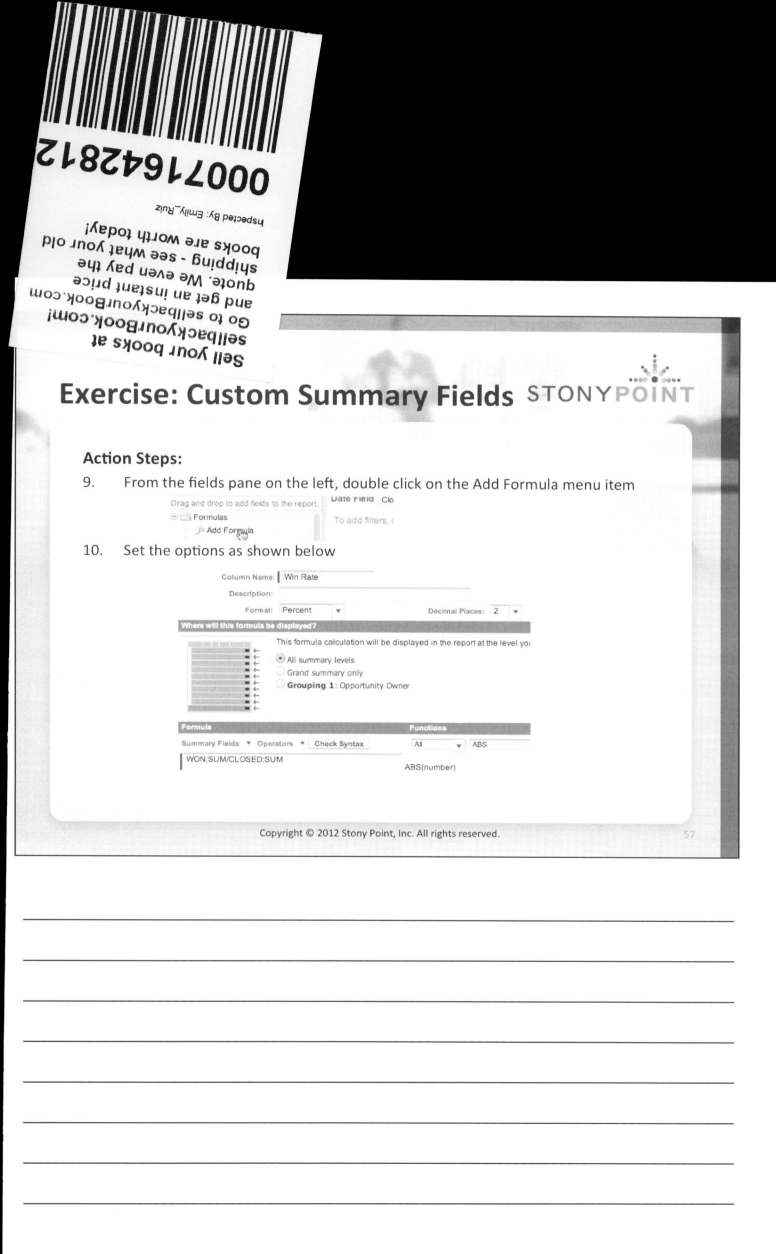

Drag and drop to add fields to the report. | Date Field | Clo

☐ Formulas
  ƒx Add Formula

To add filters. (

10. Set the options as shown below

Column Name: | Win Rate

Description:

Format: Percent ▼   Decimal Places: 2 ▼

Where will this formula be displayed?

This formula calculation will be displayed in the report at the level you

⦿ All summary levels
○ Grand summary only
○ **Grouping 1**: Opportunity Owner

Formula   **Functions**

Summary Fields ▼ Operators ▼ | Check Syntax | | All ▼ | ABS

WON:SUM/CLOSED:SUM   ABS(number)

Exercise: Custom Summary Fields

Action Steps:

11. Run the report by clicking the Run Report button
12. Save the report by clicking the Save As button
13. Name the report Win Rates
14. Make sure to save the report in the GenWatt Reports folder
15. Click the Save and Return to Report button

Question: What was your rate?

_____

_____

_____

_____

_____

_____

_____

_____

Conditional Highlighting

- Allows highlighting of summary fields on a report based on the calculated values of the summary fields
  - Only works on summary fields
- Available on Summary and Matrix reports
- Can highlight up to 3 different summary fields
- There is a maximum of 3 colors per field

_____

_____

_____

_____

_____

_____

_____

GenWatt would like to monitor the length of their sales cycles. The executives would like to be able to quickly identify if there are steps in the sales process where opportunities are stalling.

_____

_____

_____

_____

_____

_____

_____

Exercise: Conditional Highlighting  STONYPOINT

Action Steps:

1. Create a new Summary Report listing all Open Opportunity records
2. Navigate to the Reports tab and click on New Report button
3. Search for Opportunity, select the Opportunities type and create the report by clicking the Create button
4. Change the Scope to:
   a. Show: All Opportunities
   b. Opportunity Status: Open
   c. Range: All Time
5. Ensure the report has the following columns in order:
   a. Stage, Opportunity Name, Opportunity Owner, Close Date, Amount, Stage Duration
6. Change the Report Format to Summary
7. Group the Report by Stage
8. Choose to Summarize the Average of the Stage Duration field

61

61

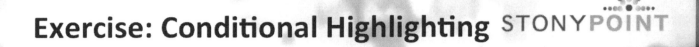

Exercise: Conditional Highlighting STONYPOINT

Action Steps:

9. Add conditional highlighting by clicking the Show button and choosing conditional highlight

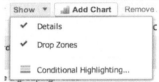

10. Set the following highlighting rules

11. Run the report
12. Save the report as Stage Duration in the GenWatt Reports folder
13. Click the Save and Return to Report button

Custom Report Type

- Used when Salesforce doesn't automatically create the Report Type needed
- Benefits:
  - With or without (outer joins)
  - Control fields available
  - Control Layout of fields available
  - Cross object fields just for reporting
    - No need to build a formula field on the object
  - Set default selections
  - Change Field Labels just for the report
- Drawback:
  - New fields must be manually added to all Custom Report Types that exist when the new field is created
  - Changing the objects in a Custom Report Type that is in use by Reports destroys all Reports built using the Custom Report Type

63

_____

_____

_____

_____

_____

_____

_____

Business Scenario: Custom Report Type

GenWatt would like a report to help identify all Accounts and Contacts. They specifically want to include Accounts that do not have any Contacts so they can begin attempting to identify contacts within the account. When they run a report based on the standard Contacts & Account report type, not all Accounts appear on the report. Only the Accounts that have Contacts appear so GenWatt can't find out what they need to know.

Build a new custom report type that will allow GenWatt to see all Accounts and show the related Contact records if they exist.

Exercise: Create Custom Report Type

STONYPOINT

Action Steps:

1. Create a new custom report type to show all Accounts and show Contacts if they exist

2. Navigate to Setup-> Create -> Report Types

3. Create a new type by clicking the New Custom Report Type button

4. Select Accounts as the Primary Object

5. Make the following selections:

   a. Report Type Label: Accounts w/wo Contacts

   b. Report Type Name: Accounts_w_wo_Contacts

   c. Description: Shows all Accounts and show related Contacts if they exist

   d. Store in Category: Accounts & Contacts

6. Check the Deployed box in the Deployment Status section

7. Add the relationships as shown on the next page

65

Exercise: Create Custom Report Type

Action Steps:

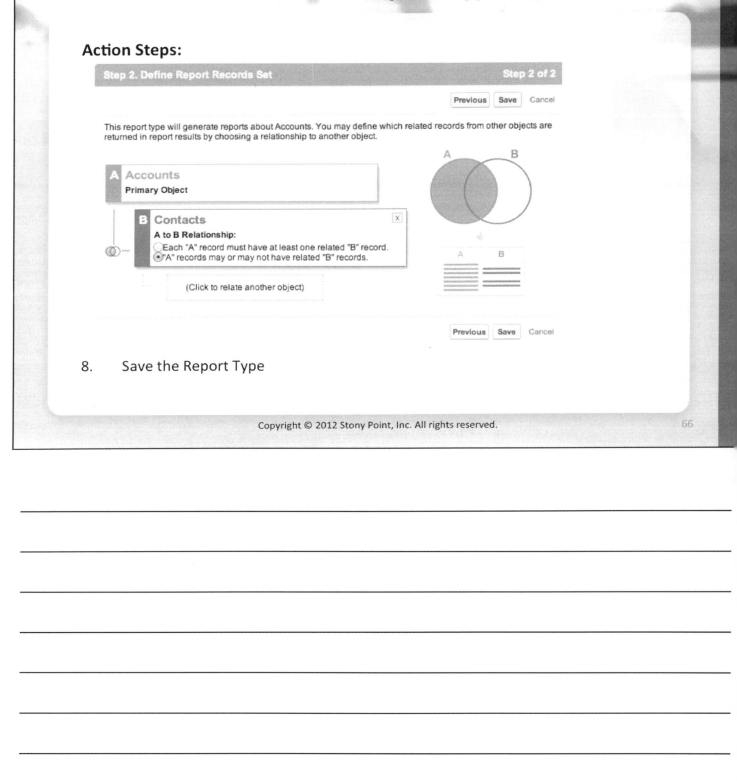

8. Save the Report Type

Exercise: Create Custom Report Type

Action Steps:

9. Edit the Report Type layout by clicking the Edit Layout button in the Fields Available for Reports section at the bottom of the page

10. Make the following fields default selections:

    a. Account Name, Account Owner, Full Name, Email, Mobile

11. Add the Account Owner's Email field using a related field via lookup

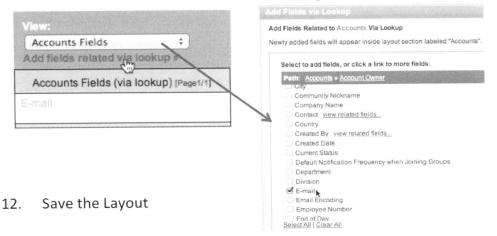

12. Save the Layout

Exercise: Create a Summary Report

Action Steps:

1. Create a new Summary Report listing all Accounts and related Contacts if they exist

2. Navigate to the Reports tab and click on New Report button

3. Search for Accounts, select the Accounts w/wo Contacts type and create the report by clicking the Create button

4. Change the Scope to:
   a. Show: All Accounts
   b. Range: All Time

5. Leave the default columns

6. Sort the report by Account Name

7. Run the report by clicking the Run Report button

8. Save the report by clicking the Save As button

9. Name the report Accounts with/without Contacts

10. Make sure to save the report in the GenWatt Reports folder

11. Click the Save and Return to Report button

Question: How many Accounts have no Contact records?

Scheduling Reports

- Run a report on a schedule and email it
- Behaviors
  - Recipients of email must be Salesforce Users
  - Can be scheduled to run daily
  - Report runs within 30 minutes of Preferred Start Time.
  - Each Report can only have 1 schedule
  - You can't create schedules for joined reports
  - Maximum of 200 scheduled reports
    - Can buy more
  - Report charts are not included in emailed reports.
    - To email a chart of the report, create a dashboard and schedule a dashboard refresh.
    - Maximum size for emailed reports is 10 MB.

Exercise: Schedule a Report

Action Steps:

1. Navigate to the Reports tab
2. Select an existing report and run it
3. While viewing the report, click the Run Report drop down menu to schedule the report

4. On the report scheduling screen, choose the recipients, the frequency, the schedule and the preferred start time.
5. Save the Report Schedule

Dashboard Overview

 What is a Dashboard?

- A Dashboard is a graphical representation of data within Salesforce
- A Dashboard is made up of charts, graphs, tables and gauges called Components
  - Can also include Visual Force pages as Components
- A Dashboard can have up to 20 Components
- Each Component is linked to a custom Report which populates the data within the Component
  - When a User clicks on a Component, they are able to drill down into the Report behind the Component
- Dashboards are not necessarily real time data

_____

_____

_____

_____

_____

_____

_____

Creating Dashboards

- The steps to create a Dashboard are:
    1. Develop a custom Report for each Component
    2. Save each custom Report to a public Report Folder
    3. Create a Dashboard and save it to a public Dashboard Folder
    4. Add Components to the Dashboard
    5. Determine who the Running User of the Dashboard should be
    6. Schedule the Dashboard to Refresh periodically

_____

_____

_____

_____

_____

_____

_____

Exercise: Create a Dashboard Folder

Action Steps:

1. Create a new Dashboard Folder to hold the GenWatt dashboards
2. Navigate to the Reports tab
3. Click on the New Dashboard Folder link

4. Choose the following options
   a. Report Folder Label: GenWatt Dashboards
   b. Folder Unique Name: GenWatt_Dashboards
   c. Public Folder Access: Read Only
   d. This folder is accessible by all users
5. Don't add any Dashboards to the folder at this time
6. Save the folder

Installing Prebuilt Dashboards

- Force.com Labs (salesforce.com Strategic Services department) has created a great set of Dashboards for Sales, Marketing, Service and Support, User Adoption

- They are FREE from the AppExchange

- In this class, we are going to install these as well as building our own

74

7

Installing Prebuilt Dashboards

1. Click on the force.com app menu in the upper right hand of the home page

2. Select ***Add AppExchange Apps...***

3. In the Search box, type in *Adoption Dashboards* and click on the magnifying glass

_____

_____

_____

_____

_____

_____

_____

Installing Prebuilt Dashboards STONYPOINT

4. Find the listing called Salesforce Adoption Dashboards and click on the link

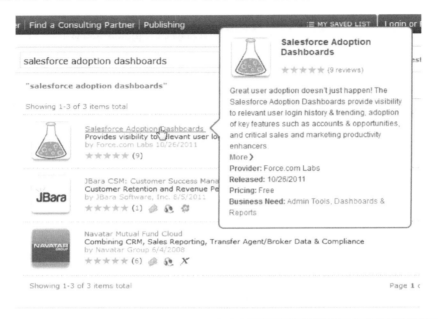

Installing Prebuilt Dashboards

5. Click on the **Get It Now** button
6. Select the prompts as shown below and click **Continue**

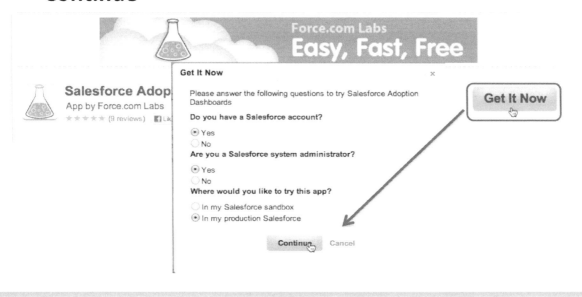

_____

_____

_____

_____

_____

_____

_____

Installing Prebuilt Dashboards STONYPOINT

7. Enter your developer edition login credentials
8. Click the **Login** button

78

_____

_____

_____

_____

_____

_____

_____

Installing Prebuilt Dashboards STONYPOINT

9. Check the checkbox to indicate you've read and agree to the terms and conditions

10. Click the **Install** button

11. If prompted, enter your password once more and click the **Submit** button

79

79

12. On the Package Installation Details step, click on the **Continue** button

13. In the Application Package API Access step, Click the **Next** button

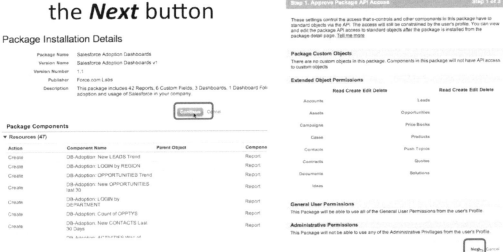

Installing Prebuilt Dashboards  STONYPOINT

14. Grant access to all users

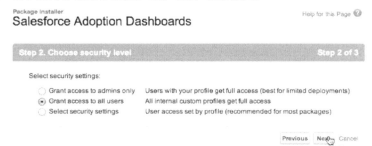

15. In the final Install Package step, click the *Install* button

_____

_____

_____

_____

_____

_____

_____

Business Scenario: Dashboard

GenWatt sales would like a quick, easy way to get a graphic representation of their sales performance.

82

_____

_____

_____

_____

_____

_____

_____

Exercise: Create a Dashboard

Action Steps:

1. Create a new Dashboard to display the key sales metrics
2. Navigate to the Reports tab and click on New Dashboard button
3. Click the Save button

Save Dashboard

Title	GenWatt Sales Dashboard
Dashboard Unique Name	GenWatt_Sales_Dashboard

Folder
To avoid exposing sensitive data to the wrong people, choose a folder visible only to the right users

Save to   GenWatt Dashboards

Save   Save and Run Dashboard   Cancel

   a. It's a good idea to save Dashboards often

4. Create a Funnel Chart for the sales pipeline
   a. From the Components tab on the left, drag a Funnel Chart component into the column on the far right
   b. From the Data Sources tab on the left, expand the Reports folder then expand the GenWatt Reports folder
   c. Drag the Open Opportunities by Stage Report and Drop it on top of the Funnel Chart component you just added in the column on the far right
   d. After the chart has finished processing, edit the Header, Title and Footer of the component as you see necessary
5. Save the Dashboard by clicking the Save button

Exercise: Create a Dashboard

Action Steps:

6.   Create a Table for the Win Rates
    a.   From the Components tab on the left, drag a Table component into the column in the center
    b.   From the Data Sources tab on the left, expand the Reports folder then expand the GenWatt Reports folder
    c.   Drag the Win Rate Report and Drop it on top of the Table component you just added in the column in the center
    d.   After the chart has finished processing, edit the properties on the component by clicking on the Wrench on the component

    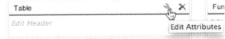

    e.   On the formatting tab, choose to Sort Rows By Value Descending
        i.   This will reorder the data to show the best performers at the top
    f.   Click OK to close the window
    g.   Edit the Header, Title and Footer of the component as you see necessary

7.   Save the Dashboard by clicking the Save button

Exercise: Create a Dashboard

Action Steps:

8.   Create a Gauge for the Win Rates

    a.   From the Components tab on the left, drag a Gauge component into the column on the left

    b.   From the Data Sources tab on the left, expand the Reports folder then expand the GenWatt Reports folder

    c.   Drag the Win Rate Report and Drop it on top of the Gauge component you just added in the left column

    d.   After the gauge has finished processing, edit the properties on the component by clicking on the Wrench on the component

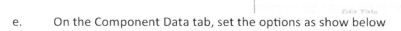

    e.   On the Component Data tab, set the options as show below

_____

_____

_____

_____

_____

_____

_____

_____

     85

Exercise: Create a Dashboard

Action Steps:

f. On the Formatting tab, set the options as shown below

g. Save the changes by clicking OK

h. Edit the Header, Title and Footer of the component as you see necessary

9. Save the Dashboard by clicking the Save button then run it by clicking the Save & Close button

_____

_____

_____

_____

_____

_____

_____

Running User

- The User whose permissions will be used to populate all Components on the Dashboard
- Two Types:
  - Specified User
    - A specific User whose credentials are always used to run the Dashboard
    - Data is saved with Dashboard and must be refreshed
    - Allows CEO who has all access to all records the ability to publish key summary metrics without exposing the detail to everyone
    - Note: Users with a Salesforce Platform or Salesforce Platform One user license can only view a dashboard if the dashboard running user also has the same license type.
      - Consider creating separate dashboards for users with different license types.
  - Logged In User
    - Dashboard will automatically run and populate the Components using only the data that the current User is able to view
    - Limited amount allowed
- In order for the Dashboard to work properly, the Running User must have read access to the Dashboard Folder and all Report Folders being used to populate Components in the Dashboard

87

Scheduling Dashboards

- Refresh a Dashboard on a schedule
  - This is necessary to ensure that the data is updated
- Behaviors
  - Can be emailed but does not need to be
  - Recipients of email must be Salesforce Users
  - Charts are included in the email
    - Users can click on Charts to drill through to the underlying report
  - Can be scheduled to run daily
  - Refresh runs within 30 minutes of Preferred Start Time.
  - Each Dashboard can only have 1 schedule
  - Maximum of 200 scheduled Dashboards
    - Can buy more

Knowledge Check

1. How do you secure List Views?
2. How do you secure Reports?
3. How do you secure Dashboards?
4. What is a Report Type?
5. What are the four Report Formats?
6. How many components can be included in a single Dashboard?
7. What Report Formats can be included in Dashboards?
8. True or False: Dashboard Components are always driven off Reports?
9. In order to use a Report to drive a Dashboard Component, what must be true about the report?
10. If you wanted to schedule the same report to run twice daily, what would you need to do?

89

_____

_____

_____

_____

_____

_____

_____

Survey

Please take this time to fill out the course survey.

Your instructor will send an email with login instructions.

Question and Answer

Please take this time to ask the instructor questions on what you've learned in class.

For additional training, please visit www.stonyp.com.

_____

_____

_____

_____

_____

_____

_____

Made in the USA
San Bernardino, CA
13 February 2013